Sports Illustrated KIDS

MY FIRST BOOK OF FOOTBALL

It's **SCRIMMAGE**, dude. And no, we're stretching before we get started.

Are we at the line of spinach?

By Beth Bugler and Mark Bechtel

A ROOKIE Book

Illustrations by Bill Hinds

Football is an action-packed game played by

TWO TEAMS

of (mostly) big guys who try to score as many points as possible.

Each team has
11 PLAYERS
on the field at a time.

The game is divided into

FOUR QUARTERS

that are **15 MINUTES** each.

↑

Here, after the second quarter, comes

HALFTIME.

That's a short break
for everyone!

A break?
But we're just
getting started!

The **FIELD** is **100 YARDS** long.

That's like **8** school buses in a row!

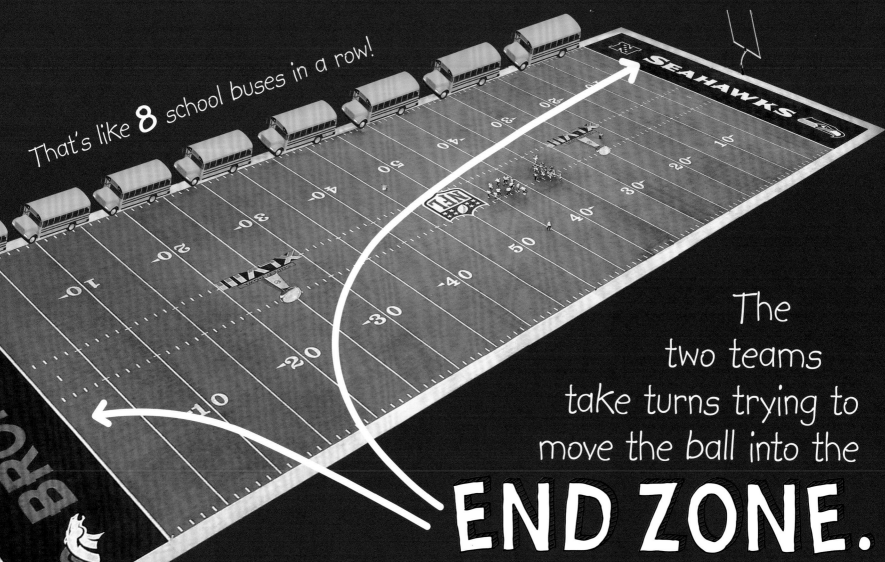

The two teams take turns trying to move the ball into the

END ZONE.

This is where players score and the points add up!

And where I bust out my **end zone dance!!**

To determine which team gets the ball first, the captains and the officials get together for a friendly, old-school

COIN TOSS.

The captain of the visiting team gets to call "heads" or "tails." Whoever wins the toss gets to decide if they want the ball.

Heads, heads, heads . . .

Excuse me, I'll need that **QUARTER** back.

TIME
15:00

A player from the other team catches the ball and runs with it toward the end zone until . . .

I got it!
I got it!
I **DON'T** got it!

. . . he gets

TACKLED!

Oof! That means he's
brought to the ground
by an opponent.

TIMBER!!

Now the two teams each gather in a

HUDDLE

to go over their strategy.

This is the

COACH. ⟶

He tells the guys which plays to run.

This is the

QUARTERBACK.

He's the big cheese, the main man
who calls the shots on the field
when his team has the ball.

Did I forget to lock the house this morning?

The players with the
ball are called the

OFFENSE.

Can we get this
show on the road? My
back is **killing** me!

The coach calls a running play.

The QB will

HAND OFF

the ball to a running back,
who takes off down the field.

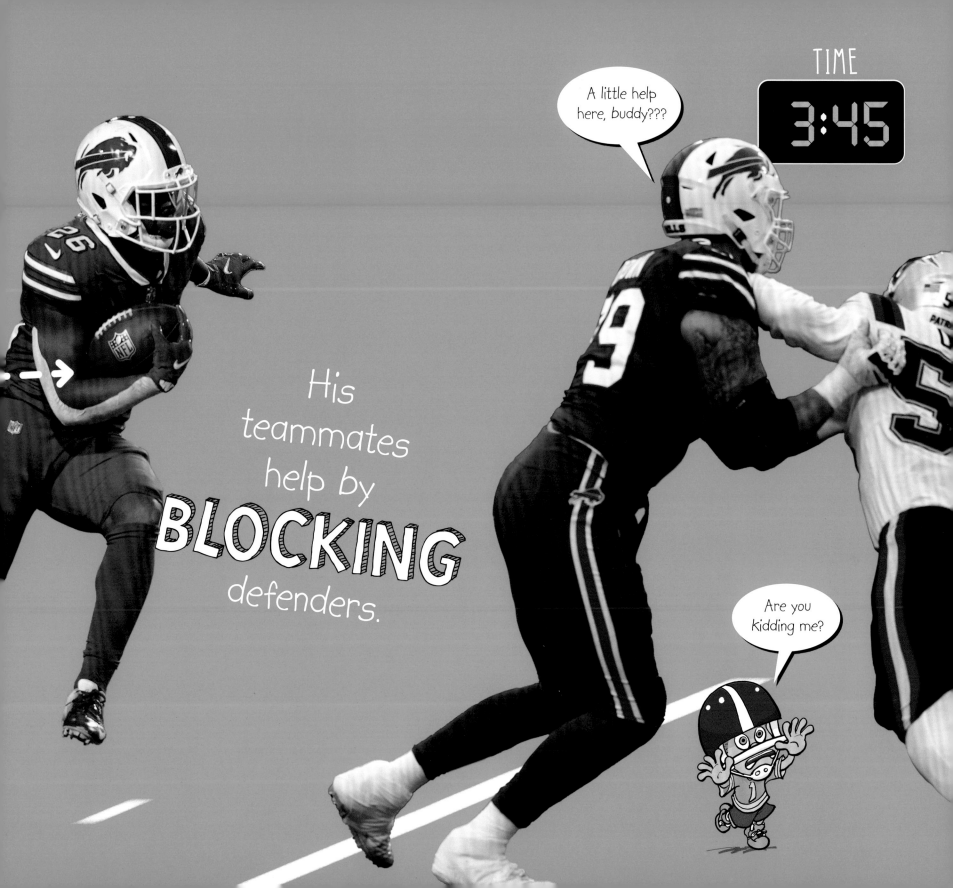

QUARTER

2ND

The offense has four chances, called DOW

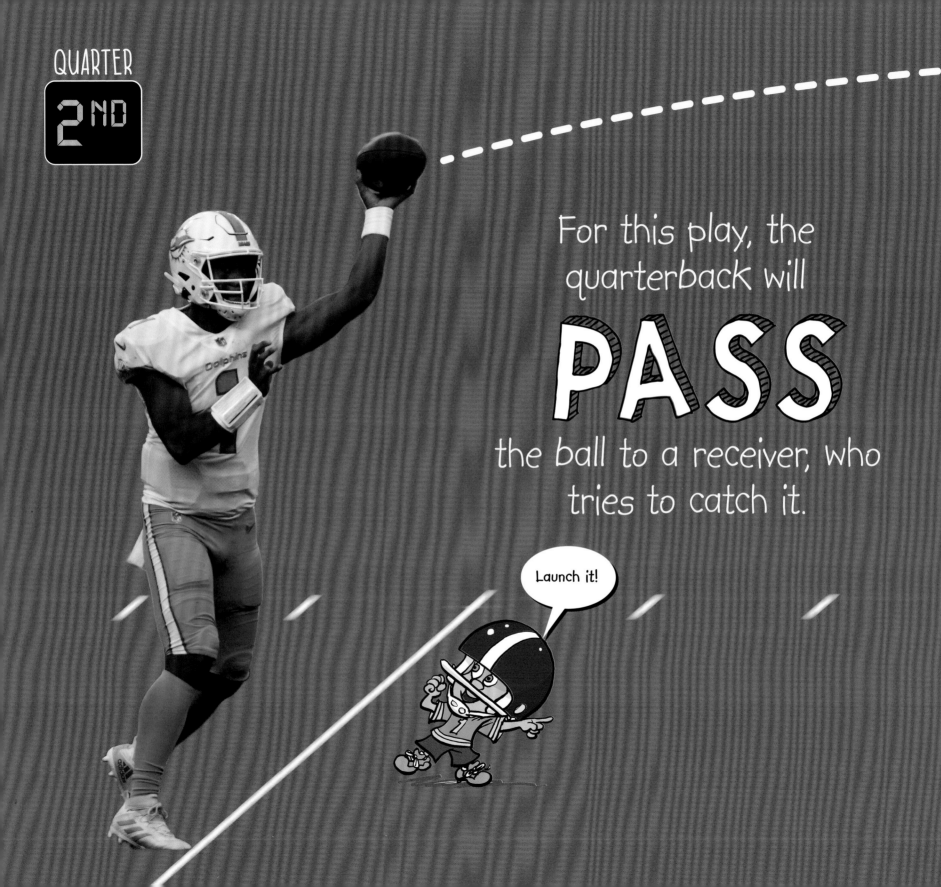

QUARTER

2ND

Caught it! And he got
enough yards for a

FIRST DOWN!

The offense gets to keep driving
the football toward the end zone.

This way?

But if the offense gets stuck and it's

FOURTH DOWN,

they have a **big** decision to make.
If they run or pass and don't make
a first down, they lose the ball.

However, if they are close enough to the end zone, they can try a

FIELD GOAL.

The kicker sends the ball through the goalposts—his team gets three points!

Look at the clock! It's almost time for that break, right?

TIME

3:15

HALFT

O.K., everyone!
While the coaches talk
to the players in the
locker room, it's your
chance to take care of:

1.

Getting a snack.

IME!!!

2.  Stretching your legs.

3.  Whatever else needs to be taken care of.

At the beginning of the

SECOND HALF,

the team that got the ball to start the game kicks off.

QUARTER

3RD

Oops!
The QB missed his receiver.
It's an

INCOMPLETE PASS.

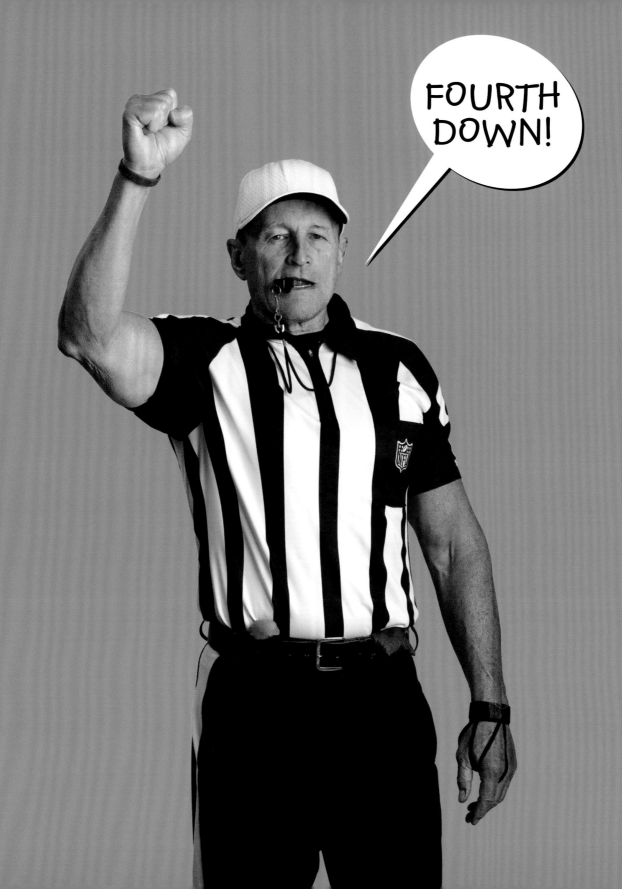

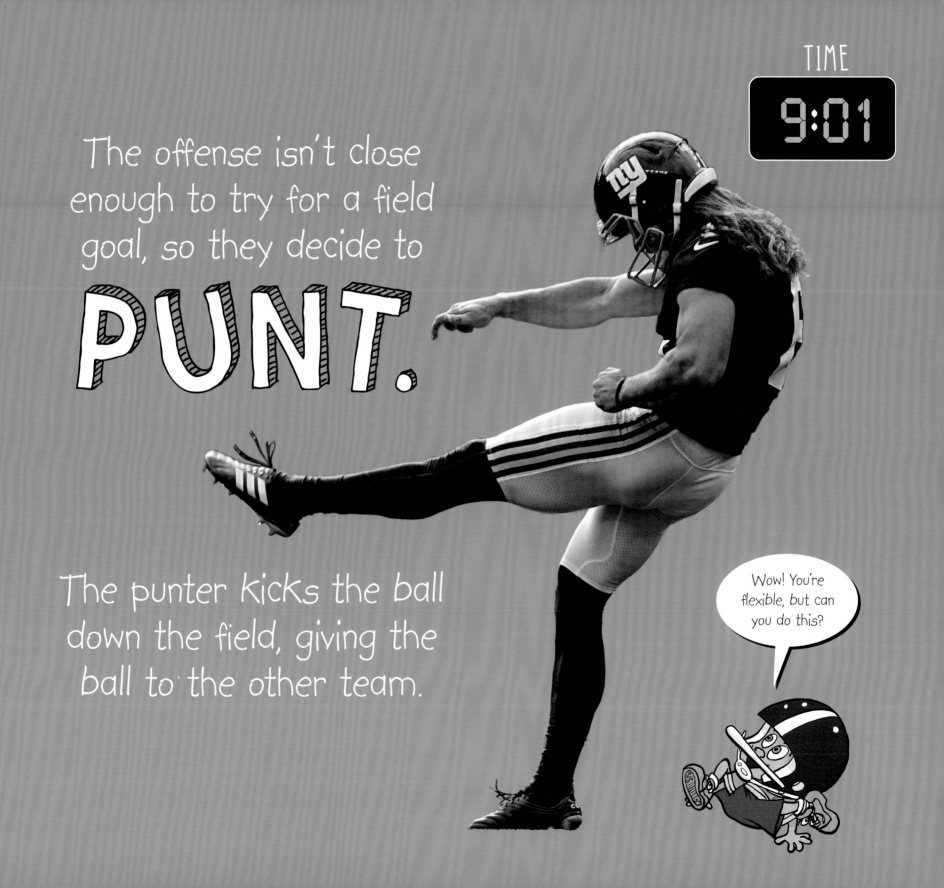

The offense isn't close enough to try for a field goal, so they decide to

PUNT.

The punter kicks the ball down the field, giving the ball to the other team.

TIME
9:01

Wow! You're flexible, but can you do this?

Oh, no! It's a

FUMBLE!

The ball carrier
dropped the ball.

Whoopsie
daisy!

QUARTER

4TH

That was a nice play!

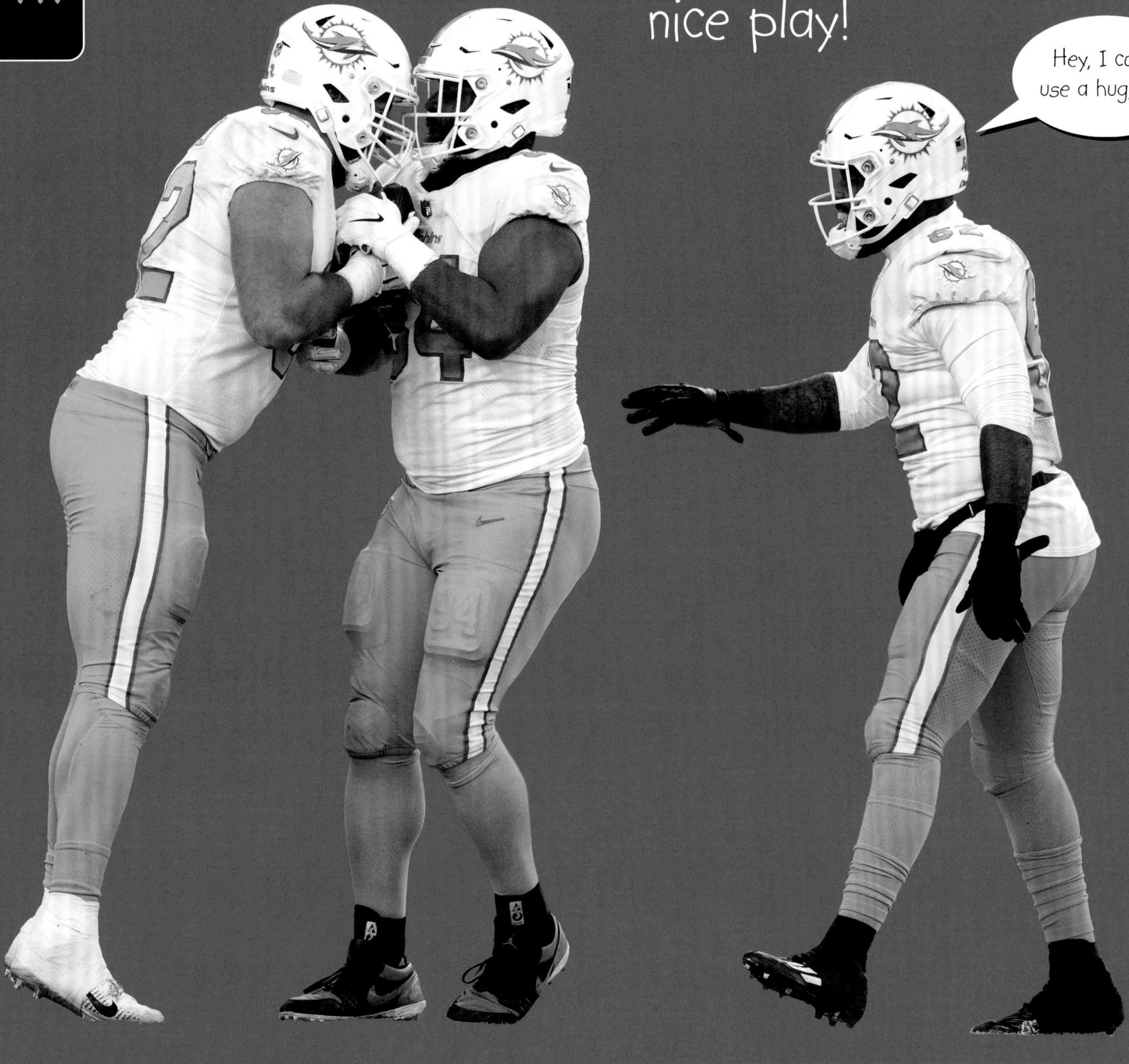

But wait. What's that

FLAG

on the field? An official threw it
there because someone broke
a rule and committed a

PENALTY.

The guilty team is punished.
If it's the defense, the ball is moved
closer to the end zone. If it's the
offense, the ball is
moved farther away.

And no video
games for a
week!

The quarterback
is trying to complete
another pass.
Yikes! It's an

INTERCEPTION!

A player for the other team caught the ball.

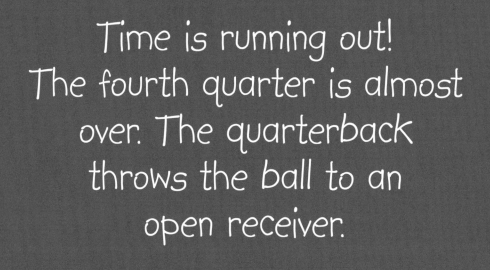

Time is running out!
The fourth quarter is almost
over. The quarterback
throws the ball to an
open receiver.

He catches it, and
he's heading toward
the end zone.

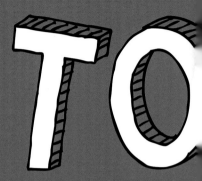

It's a

UCHDOWN!

He made it into the end zone.
That's six points! And his team will get
a chance to score one more point if they
kick the ball through the goalposts!

But first . . .

The clock hits zero.

GAME OVER!

It's time to celebrate!

That was **awesome!** I can't wait to do it again. But next time I'm bringing my umbrella!

PHOTO CREDITS, in order
Page 1: AP Images; Page 2: AP Images; Page 3: Simon Bruty; Page 5: John Moore/Getty Images; Page 7: Bill Frakes; Page 8: Brad Mangin; Page 11: Erick W. Rasco; Page 12: Simon Bruty; Page 13: David E. Klutho; Page 14: AP Images; Page 15: AP Images; Page 16: Simon Bruty; Page 17: Erick W. Rasco (Singletary), Simon Bruty; Page 18: David E. Klutho; Page 19: AP Images (Prescott), Simon Bruty (referee); Page 20: Carlos M. Saavedra; Page 21: AP Images; Page 22: John W. McDonough; Page 24: Kohjiro Kinno; Page 29: AP Images; Page 30: AP Images; Page 31: AP Images; Page 32: John W. McDonough; Page 33: Erick W. Rasco; Page 34: AP Images; Page 35: AP Images; Page 36: AP Images; Page 38: Erick W. Rasco; Page 39: Greg Nelson; Page 40: Greg Nelson; Page 41: Greg Nelson; Page 42: Al Tielemans; Page 44: John W. McDonough; Page 47: AP Images; Back cover: Erick W. Rasco.

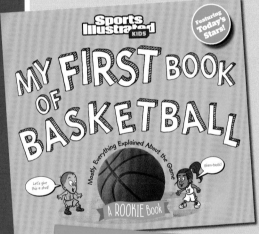
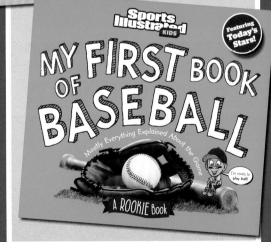